50 fabulous ways to

decorate
your garden

~Bouquet Garnis~

50 fabulous ways to
decorate
your garden

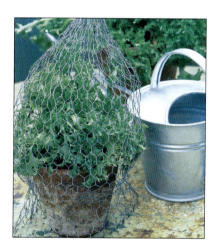

Transform your outside space with easy step-by-step projects and creative ideas

Tessa Evelegh

southwater

This edition is published by Southwater

Southwater is an imprint of Anness Publishing Ltd
Hermes House, 88–89 Blackfriars Road, London SE1 8HA
tel. 020 7401 2077; fax 020 7633 9499
www.southwaterbooks.com; info@anness.com

© Anness Publishing Ltd 2005

UK agent: The Manning Partnership Ltd
6 The Old Dairy, Melcombe Road, Bath BA2 3LR
tel. 01225 478444; fax 01225 478440
sales@manning-partnership.co.uk

UK distributor: Grantham Book Services Ltd
Isaac Newton Way, Alma Park Industrial Estate
Grantham, Lincs NG31 9SD
tel. 01476 541080; fax 01476 541061
orders@gbs.tbs-ltd.co.uk

North American agent/distributor: National Book Network
4501 Forbes Boulevard, Suite 200, Lanham, MD 20706
tel. 301 459 3366; fax 301 429 5746
www.nbnbooks.com

Australian agent/distributor: Pan Macmillan Australia
Level 18, St Martins Tower,
31 Market St, Sydney, NSW 2000
tel. 1300 135 113; fax 1300 135 103
customer.service@macmillan.com.au

New Zealand agent/distributor: David Bateman Ltd
30 Tarndale Grove, Off Bush Road, Albany, Auckland
tel. (09) 415 7664; fax (09) 415 8892

Previously published as part of a larger volume,
Decorating Your Garden.

Publisher Joanna Lorenz
Editorial Director Helen Sudell
Editors Sarah Ainley and Elizabeth Woodland
Copy Editor Beverley Jollands
Editorial Reader Joy Wotton
Design Ian Sandom
Cover Design Whitelight Design Associates
Photography Debbie Patterson
Production Controller Claire Rae

1 3 5 7 9 10 8 6 4 2

PICTURE CREDITS
Jonathan Buckley p34tr; John Freeman p41t, b;
Michelle Garrett p20, 21, 42, 43, 44, 45, 51, 54, 55, 60, 61, 74, 75, 76,
77, 86, 87, 83, 92, 93, 94l, bl, 95; Tim Imrie p16, 17, 24, 40bl, 50bl, 68,
69, 70, 71, 72, 73; Simon McBride p37bl; David Parmiter p78, 79;
Spike Powell p10, 11tl, tr, 14, 15, 24r, 25t, 30br;
The Garden Picture Library p11b; Peter Williams p26, 27, 88, 89, 94tr;
Polly Wreford p9, 13tr, 25b.

ACKNOWLEDGEMENTS
The author and publishers would like to thank the following artists
for contributing the projects featured in this book:
Helen Baird, Stephanie Donaldson, Mijke Gesthuizen,
Andrew Gillmore, Karin Hossack, Gilly Love, Mary Maguire,
Cleo Mussi, Andrew Newton-Cox, Jenny Norton, Liz Wagstaff,
Wendy Wilbraham and Peter Williams.

CONTENTS

INTRODUCTION

Stylish gardens don't have to be hard work. The key is to take your interior decorating ideas and skills and to adapt them to your outdoor room. This could be as simple as a splash of paint applied to chairs and tables, or an imaginative choice of colours in your planting scheme. You can add decorative touches such as sculptures, ornaments, plant containers, lanterns and lighting, as well as other accessories, in the same way as you would do indoors. This book shows you how easy it is to create a great garden with very little effort.

The smallest garden can become the most successful decorated garden room for all the family if it is well planned. If your garden is large, you could just decorate the patio area for entertaining to begin with and work round to other areas when you have the time and the funds. Large or small, the best way to get the most from any garden is to set up a comfortable seating and/or eating area, so it's always ready for relaxing and entertaining. No need to wait for high summer before you sit outside: if everything is at hand, it's easy to carry out food or drinks, even on fine spring days.

■ ABOVE
A lantern can be suspended from the same bracket as a hanging basket, where its soft light will enhance the flowers magically after sunset.

THE BASIC DECORATING
The quickest way to introduce all-year colour into the garden is to paint it on. No worrying about what will flower when, or how to keep the colour going through the winter – it's there for keeps. Adding colour in the garden with paint and stain has become easier in recent years as there's a much wider choice of exterior paints and stains. Where once we were limited to pine green or various shades of brown, now turquoise greens, pinks, blues and lilacs are being added to the repertoire available. Use it to paint fences, trellis work and buildings, and to add to the impact, you can plan the planting to complement the colour scheme.

■ LEFT
Simple enamel tableware and a wire "coffee pot" make unusual containers for strawberry plants, pelargoniums, pansies, verbenas and daisy-like, yellow zinnia.

■ RIGHT
Three colours of paint have been used to brighten this outdoor setting. The bold use of colour, with the cushions and the display of plants on the wall, gives the corner a strong Mediterranean feel.

SOFT FURNISHINGS

Once the basic decorating is done, you can begin to choose the soft furnishings, which, in the garden, is the planting.

For instant colour, which you can use to supplement the planting, pot seasonal bedding plants into containers. These can be used to decorate the patio, as a focal point in the garden, or even placed in the borders to boost the colour between seasons.

Buy young plants from the garden centre that are already showing colour and plant them in pots, adding fertilizer to be sure of a splashy show. Keep them moist and deadhead them regularly for a long flowering season. The advantage of containers is that once they have finished flowering they can be moved to a more secluded part of the garden, while others, coming into bloom, can be moved to centre stage.

DECORATIVE FEATURES

Mosaics make perfect all-weather outdoor art, and can be used as pictures, sculptures or even to decorate furniture. Scarecrows can be outdoor sculpture, as can piles of pots, groups of containers and old tools. Bird baths and birdhouses become ornaments, as do painted pots and wind chimes. Garden lighting adds its own special atmosphere. Well-placed candles and lanterns create a beautiful night-time display. Stamp your style on your garden using all of these, perhaps keeping to a colour theme for continuity.

FURNISHING THE GARDEN

Although the garden furniture is really the finishing touch to the garden, it can also be one of the first things you do. Even if you don't have the time or the budget to make over the garden, if you do nothing else, it's worth making a comfortable seating area so that everything is in place for relaxing in the garden – be it reading a book on your own or inviting friends over for a meal. If you're planning the garden from scratch, you may like to think about built-in furniture – a bench under a pergola, for example. If not, invest in all-weather furniture that doesn't have to be dragged in and out every day. It doesn't have to be expensive, though it does need to be comfortable. Add cushions and throws to any that falls short of the mark.

You can give the seating area a relaxing ambience by aiming to stimulate all the senses. Glean visual inspiration from the pages of this book and add perfume by choosing scented varieties of plant, such as honeysuckle, old-fashioned roses, summer jasmine and tobacco plants. Smell stimulates the tastebuds, too, so add in some sweet-smelling herbs such as marjoram, sage or rosemary and potted summer fruits, such as strawberries. Bring on the music with wind chimes or a water feature, and add soft feathery foliage such as love-in-a-mist for that touchy-feely element.

IN A NUTSHELL

Think of your garden as a place to relax: plan it to suit you and your lifestyle; decorate it as boldly as you would your home using paint, stain, flowers and foliage for your favourite colour palette; furnish it for comfort; add finishing touches, scents and sound for ambience; then sit back and enjoy.

DECORATIVE GARDEN FURNITURE

To make your garden a space you can really live in, it must be furnished: choose comfortable-looking pieces that will tempt you to go outside, kick off your shoes and relax, soaking up the sun or cooling off in the shade.

A vast range of garden furniture is available but you can narrow down your options by deciding whether you want your furnishings to be permanent fixtures or moveable feasts. Lightweight garden furniture is inexpensive but often lacks glamour, and makes a good candidate for customized paint treatments, or embellishments with cushions and cloths. Wooden or stone furniture is expensive to buy, but it makes a long-term investment that will add an architectural dimension to your garden all through the year.

Garden furniture performs a practical function, but it is also decorative and can be as quirky as you like. For a really original touch, why not revitalize an old or uninspiring chair or table with your own beautiful mosaic design?

■ ABOVE
The relaxed elegance of this classic garden seat makes it a feature in itself.

■ OPPOSITE
A simple slatted chair is easily customized with a few coats of paint.

CHOOSING GARDEN FURNITURE

There is an enormous range of furniture available for the garden, from folding metal or canvas chairs, which can be stored in a shed and just brought out when they are needed, to whole suites of hardwood dining furniture. While you may not want your garden to be cluttered with enough chairs to seat a crowd all the time, a few carefully placed permanent fixtures, such as a weatherproof hardwood bench, a metal table and a few chairs on the patio or an inviting wooden bench under an arbour, all play an important role in the garden's structure and make it look especially welcoming and lived-in.

If you fancy a quick coffee break in a brief burst of spring sunshine, you won't want to spend time searching in the shed for a chair to sit on, and a plain wooden bench that lives all year long in the garden is just the place for a breather during a heavy digging session on a cold winter's day.

For furniture that is to be left outside all year, choose durable materials such as painted metal or hardwood (from sustainable sources). Softer woods should be hardened and will need treating with preservative, which will need renewing at least once a year for it to remain effective. Plastic furniture needs little maintenance except for washing, but it has a limited life outdoors and will eventually become brittle and easily breakable.

Other highly decorative materials that are also comfortable include wicker and Lloyd loom, but these are not weatherproof and will need to be stored in a garden shed, garage or conservatory when not in use.

■ RIGHT
This unique piece of furniture, half-chair and half-sculpture, is made from driftwood and fencing stakes, and is perfect for an outdoor setting.

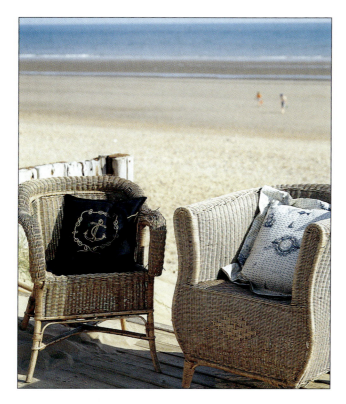

■ RIGHT
Wicker furniture
is comfortable,
especially if
cushions are
added to fit
the seats. It
will look good
in any garden
setting. Used
outside in
summer, it will
weather to a
subtle natural
shade, or it can
be painted for a
brighter look.

■ BELOW
Traditional slatted folding chairs look
pretty in the garden and make perfect
seating for an al fresco dinner party.

■ RIGHT
Metal furniture
is robust enough
to need very
little mainten-
ance, and can
be kept outside
throughout
the year.

GARDEN CHAIRS

Furnishing the garden gives you somewhere to sit and relax and, at the same time, adds to the architectural element of the garden. Some furniture – a traditional stone seat, for example – is designed to be an almost permanent part of the garden; certainly stone seats are not moved with regularity.

Architecturally, permanent seating provides another step up visually, with its legs equal to balustrades. While such wonderful garden fixtures aren't really within most people's budgets, a similar role is played by old wooden garden benches, which, as they weather to a soft green-tinged grey, take on a permanent air as part of the garden architecture.

Single benches exude a peaccful air, probably because they are not conducive to conversation but are more for sitting and contemplating. Love seats, designed in an S-shape, are far more sociable since the occupants sit facing each other. Groups of chairs around an outdoor table represent social times in the garden, whether you are simply eating outside with the family, taking tea with a friend or having an evening party.

In high summer, there is nothing more enjoyable than lounging around in the garden, and this is when the softer, more reclining types of chair, including canvas deck-chairs and directors' chairs, come into their own. The lounger is the lotus-eater's dream – more day-bed than chair. Wood-slatted steamer chairs were the original loungers, designed for use on long voyages. Their modern equivalents – in wood, metal, or plastic – are fitted with upholstered cushions. Hammocks are another kind of day-bed, and, gently swaying between a pair of trees, they would challenge anyone to stay awake.

■ BELOW
This witty, plastic-covered Louis XIV chair offers indoor elegance outside.

■ ABOVE
Softly weathered wooden furniture fits easily into almost any garden setting.

■ LEFT
This modern wrought-iron furniture is inspired by the French styles of the last century, the elegant lightweight lines of which are now enjoying a revival.

■ RIGHT

Furniture makes its own contribution to the look of the garden and, if it's not being used to sit on, it can make an ideal backdrop for decorative garden "pieces".

■ BELOW

Elaborate cast-iron furniture became a favourite in Victorian times, and its popularity has not waned. Its price, however, means most people will have to settle for an imitation, rather than the real thing.

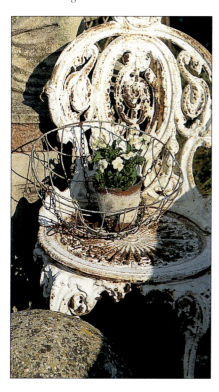

■ RIGHT

An old Lloyd loom chair was given a fresh look a few years ago with two shades of blue spray car paint. Even though the finish is now rather worn, the chair exudes a comfortable, cottage-garden feel.

STRING AND DRIFTWOOD CHAIR

You can transform an ordinary chair into something quite special by binding it with jute or garden string and attaching pieces of driftwood collected from the beach. Here, awkward joins are decorated with pieces of flotsam and jetsam, and two "horns" give a dramatic shape to the chair back. Making or changing furniture can be just a matter of using what is at hand. String is hardwearing, cheap, and gives this chair a tactile quality. Other decorative materials include bark, twigs or shells, collected on walks or at the beach.

1 Cut jute or string into manageable lengths and roll these into small balls. Glue the end of a string ball firmly to the top of the chair. You will need to do this each time you start a new ball.

2 Run a thin line of glue along the back of the chair to secure the string. Starting at one end, pull the string taut as you wrap it around the chair.

TOOLS AND MATERIALS
....
ball of jute or garden string

scissors

glue gun

chair

pieces of driftwood

3 Make two criss-cross patterns along the middle of the chair back to decorate. Hold them in place with glue.

4 Glue the driftwood to the top of the chair and secure with string. To finish off, knot and bind the string underneath.

■ RIGHT
Revive an old chair by taking a fresh look at everyday materials.

SEA-WEATHERED DIRECTOR'S CHAIR

This aging technique instantly transforms furniture from new to old, imbuing the wood with an interesting weathered quality and allowing it to blend perfectly into its outdoor surroundings. Getting away from a pristine paint surface and acquiring an old, worn look makes furniture more comfortable to live with and more relaxing to look at.

TOOLS AND MATERIALS

director's chair

scrubbing brush

bucket

soapy water

cloth

masking tape

household candle

emulsion (latex) paint in pale blue and white

paintbrushes

sandpaper

matt acrylic varnish

1 Remove the fabric from the chair and scrub the wood with soapy water. Wipe down with a dry cloth. Let dry.

2 Cover all the metal attachments with masking tape. Rub the wood with a candle, concentrating on the areas that would naturally show wear, such as the edges and corners. Dilute the pale blue emulsion (latex) 3:1 with water and paint over the chair frame. Leave to dry.

■ **BELOW**
Director's chairs are inexpensive, portable and easy to store – turn yours into furniture that's worth a second look with a simple distressing technique.

3 Rub over the paint with sandpaper to reveal the wood beneath, then rub all over with the candle again. Dilute the white emulsion 3:1 with water and paint the chair frame. Leave to dry.

4 Rub with sandpaper to reveal areas of wood and the blue paint. Seal with matt varnish, let dry and replace the fabric.

CRAZY PAVING CHAIR

This old chair, found rejected and battered in a junk shop, has been transformed into an exciting, unusual piece of furniture. It is covered in tesserae cut from a selection of china, and it's important to be aware that a large three-dimensional object like this requires a deceptively large amount of mosaic to cover it, so you would be lucky to find enough china of a single pattern. Here, the problem has been solved by using slightly different designs to cover different sections of the chair.

■ OPPOSITE
Applying mosaic to an old chair turns it into a beguilingly original piece of furniture and a focal point in the garden.

TOOLS AND MATERIALS

chair
2cm/¾in plywood
paint stripper
coarse-grade sandpaper
paintbrush
PVA (white) glue
wood glue
cement-based tile adhesive
flexible (putty) knife
pencil or chalk
large selection of old china
tile nippers
powdered tile grout
rubber gloves
stiff nailbrush
soft cloth

1 If the chair has a padded seat, remove it and replace it with a piece of plywood cut to fit the frame. Strip off any paint or varnish and rub down with coarse sandpaper. Paint the whole chair with diluted PVA (white) glue.

2 When the surface is dry, stick the seat in place with wood glue and fill any gaps with cement-based tile adhesive.

3 Draw a design or motifs on any large flat surfaces of the chair, using simple shapes that are easy to follow such as this flower.

4 Select china with colours and patterns to suit your design. Using tile nippers, cut the china into the appropriate sizes and shapes.

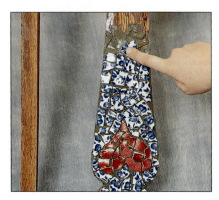

5 Spread cement-based tile adhesive within the areas of your design and press the china tesserae firmly into it.

6 Working on small areas at a time, tile the rest of the chair. Where one section of wood meets another, change the pattern of the china. Cut the china into thin slivers to tile the edges of the chair. Leave to dry for at least 24 hours.

7 Using a flexible (putty) knife, grout the mosaic with the tile adhesive. Wearing rubber gloves, rub the grout over the flat surfaces, cleaning off the excess as you work. Leave to dry.

8 When the grout is completely dry, sand off any excess cement with sandpaper or a stiff nailbrush. Polish with a soft cloth to buff up the china.

A LICK OF PAINT

Co-ordinating furniture with its surroundings helps to give the garden a harmonious ambience. By painting old furniture, you can also keep the costs down, as you can pick up bargain pieces from junk shops or simply rejuvenate old kitchen chairs that are due for replacement. And you can be sure of perfect toning as paints come in literally hundreds of shades. These chairs were most unprepossessing when they were picked up: the slatted ones were peeling and the Tyrolean-style chair was finished with a tired old varnish.

■ OPPOSITE
Clashing Caribbean colours of pink and tangerine make for a lively look in a brightly coloured garden.

■ BELOW
Taupe and white make an elegant combination for a chair with Italian-style flair. It is an ideal finish for a garden that features a lot of natural wood tones.

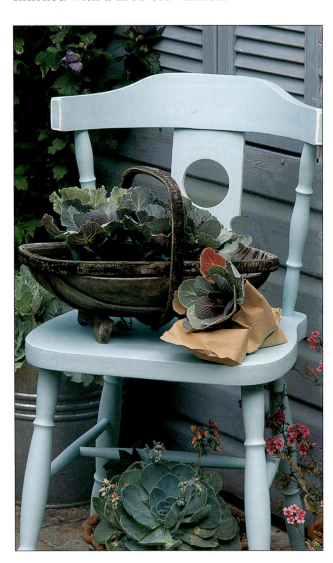

■ ABOVE
This Tyrolean-style chair is given a bright, modern finish to team with the painted shed wall behind. It also co-ordinates well with silver-grey foliage and lipstick-pink flowers.

WEATHERING AND DISTRESSING

When looking around antique shops that specialize in old garden furniture, it can be quite shocking to see the prices charged for these items. Simple folding chairs, once used in their thousands in public parks, are now desirable objects with their faded paintwork and weathered wood, and they fetch premium prices. A far less expensive alternative is to buy new hardwood folding chairs and do a bit of instant weathering yourself. Four chairs transformed in this way will cost about the same as one antique chair. The weathered effect is achieved by sanding down the surface, rubbing with wax, then painting and rubbing down again. When the chair is left out in the garden, nature will continue the weathering process, and within a season you will have your own set of heirlooms.

TOOLS AND MATERIALS

folding wooden garden chair

medium-grade sandpaper

household candle

white emulsion (latex) paint

paintbrush

wire (steel) wool

1 Sandpaper the surface of the chair to make a key so that the paint adheres. Rub over the surface randomly with the candle, applying the wax thickly on the edges and corners.

2 Paint the chair with several coats of white emulsion (latex) paint, using random strokes, and leave to dry.

3 When the paint is dry, rub the paint-work with wire (steel) wool to remove the paint from the waxed areas, so that the wood is showing. Wipe the chair with a damp cloth to clean away the dust, and leave to dry.

■ OPPOSITE
Charmingly weathered and worn, this wooden chair looks as if it has been standing in the garden for years.

DECORATIVE DECK-CHAIRS

There is little in the way of garden furniture to beat the practicality of deck-chairs. They have a traditional, comfortable look, and with the occasional new cover they will last more than a lifetime. You can buy striped deck-chair canvas and simply nail it on, but why not go a step or two further and add some pattern to a plain canvas? It really is not difficult, even if you have never considered yourself to be an expert with a paintbrush. One of these designs was made with a ready-cut stencil and the other with tracings of traditional bird motifs from copyright-free or clip art collections.

"INDIAN BIRDS" DESIGN

1. Wash, rinse, dry and iron the canvas to remove any dressing. Remove the deck-chair canvas and paint the frame with woodstain.

2. Trace a selection of traditional bird motifs (published in out-of-copyright collections). Using a soft pencil, scribble on the back. Place the tracing in position on the canvas and draw over the lines with a hard pencil to transfer the design.

3. Colour in the birds using soft fabric pens. For the border, measure 2cm/¾in from the edge of the canvas and place masking tape along the length. Draw a wavy line down the edge, then, with a contrasting pen, fill in the edges. Repeat for the inner borders, placing a strip of masking tape either side.

4. When the ink is dry, set it by covering with a white cloth and pressing with a hot iron, covering each part for at least 2 minutes. Use upholstery tacks or panel pins (tacks) to fix the canvas securely to the top and bottom of the chair.

"STENCILLED RUG" DESIGN

1. Prepare the canvas and the deck-chair as for the "Indian Birds" design. Plan the design.

2. Work out the areas of the design before you start. Starting with the borders, fix the stencil in position using masking tape. Load the stencil brush with paint and remove any excess on newspaper. Apply this colour through the stencil. Repeat until all areas of the colour have been painted. Let dry.

3. Reposition the stencil over the original colour and apply a fresh colour. Repeat until the design is complete. Set the paint and attach the canvas to the chair as for the "Indian Birds" design.

TOOLS AND MATERIALS

For the "Indian Birds" design:

deck-chair

1.5m/5ft length deck-chair canvas

exterior woodstain

paintbrush

soft and hard pencils

tracing paper

bird motifs from copyright-free or clip art collections

soft fabric pens in red, green, purple, yellow and blue

ruler

masking tape

white cloth

iron

dome-headed upholstery tacks or panel pins (tacks)

For the "Stencilled Rug" design:

deck-chair

1.5m/5ft length deck-chair canvas

exterior woodstain

paintbrush

ready-cut stencil

masking tape

stencil brush

stencil paints in red, ochre, olive and aqua

newspaper

white cloth

iron

dome-headed upholstery tacks

■ LEFT
Trace traditional motifs in a repeating design for the border of the canvas.

■ ABOVE
There's no need to stick to traditional deck-chair stripes. Decorate plain canvas to your own designs to make original, stylish garden chairs.

■ ABOVE
Ready-cut stencils are available in hundreds of designs and can be combined however you like to make abstract patterns.

■ ABOVE
Woodstain, a length of vivid canvas and some soft fabric pens are all you need to revitalize an old deck-chair.

■ ABOVE
Stencilling is a very quick way to create an individual design for a deck-chair.

GARDEN TABLES

A table is at the heart of a whole way of life in the garden. As long as the weather holds, it can take the place of the dining table, the kitchen worktop and the writing desk indoors. Once you have a table in the garden you will want to use it for breakfast, lunch and dinner – a light lunch, the children's tea, or an intimate supper. Meals outside, when the weather is balmy and the evenings long, are invariably happier and more relaxed, with the air of a picnic.

Choose a table that is substantial but not too huge, solid and not wobbly, and weatherproof so that it becomes a more or less permanent fixture in the garden. You can make your eating area into a garden room, defining the space with a screen of trellis, flower borders, a sheltering arbour, or banks of plants in containers. A pergola overhead will give dappled shade and a sense of privacy.

■ ABOVE
Paint a simple metal tabletop with a shell design then add a wash over the top to give it a weathered look. Varnish the surface to protect it.

■ LEFT
This design has bold lines and strong contrasts that suit the chunky crazy-paving style of the mosaic. It is worked on a plain round wooden table top, screwed to a metal base.

■ RIGHT

Mosaic makes an enduring surface for a garden table, and adds a rich colour accent to the garden as a whole.

■ BELOW

However battered by time and weather, delicate old wrought-iron furniture retains its air of refinement and goes on looking pretty in the garden.

WOODEN GARDEN TABLE

This sturdy table is ideal for the garden because the wood is already weathered and further aging will make it look even better. You can leave it out all year round without worrying about it, though an occasional coat of clear wood preservative would lengthen its life. The table top here measures 74 x 75cm/ 29 x 30in, but you can adapt the design to the size you require.

■ OPPOSITE
This rustic "occasional" table will happily live in the garden through all weathers, and would be perfect near a favourite garden seat as a place to put down a cup or glass, a book or a shady hat.

TOOLS AND MATERIALS

5 weathered planks, 74 x 15cm/ 29 x 6in

tape measure

saw

1m/39in weathered batten, 5 x 1cm/2 x ½in

electric drill

screwdriver

4cm/1½in screws

4 wooden poles and thick sticks

hammer

7.5cm/3in and 4cm/1½in nails

pencil

string

1 Lay the planks side by side. Cut two 48cm/19in lengths of batten, drill holes then screw across the planks about 7.5cm/3in in from either end to make the table top.

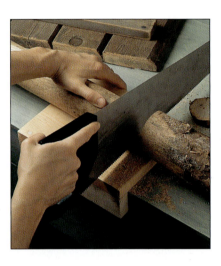

2 Saw the four poles into 90cm/36in lengths, for the legs. Cut four sticks 43cm/17in long.

3 Nail a stick a quarter of the way in from each end of each pair of legs, to make two side frames.

4 Lay the table top upside down. Centre the side frames on the battens and draw around the top of each leg.

5 Drill a pilot hole through the centre of each circle.

6 With the table top supported on one side frame, nail through into the legs. Repeat for the other side frame.

7 Cut a thick stick 62cm/25in long. Hold in place and nail it across the two side frames at the back of the table.

8 To stabilize the table, make a cross frame. Cut two lengths of stick 90cm/3ft long and nail each to a front leg and the opposite back leg. Bind with string where the sticks cross in the centre.

MOSAIC GARDEN TABLE

This striking mosaic table top is made from pieces of broken china pots and chipped decorative tiles, and with clever colour co-ordination and a simple, clear design, it makes the most attractive, weatherproof garden furniture. Although it is resilient to damp, bringing it inside over the winter will give it a longer life.

PREPARATION

To mark out the circle, tie a piece of string to a drawing pin at one end and push the pin into the centre of the plywood. Tie a pencil to the other end of the string to give you a radius of 60cm/2ft. Draw the circle and cut out using a jigsaw.

■ OPPOSITE
Mount the mosaic table top on metal or wooden legs, or simply screw it to an old circular table that is past its prime.

TOOLS AND MATERIALS

2.5cm/1in plywood at least 120cm/4ft square

string

drawing pin

pencil

jigsaw

wood primer

paintbrush

tile nippers

large selection of broken china

tile adhesive

tile grout

grout colour

rubber gloves

washing-up brush

cloth

1 Draw the design on the plywood circle, adjusting the length of string to draw concentric circles.

2 Prime the table with wood primer and leave to dry.

3 Use tile nippers to cut the broken china into pieces to fit the design and try it out on the table top. Use motifs on the china as focal points in the design.

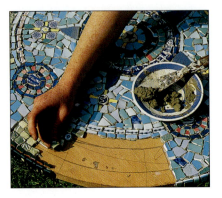

4 When the design is complete, work across the table top a section at a time, "buttering" each piece of china with adhesive and sticking it in position.

5 Mix the grout with the colour and, wearing rubber gloves, use your fingers to work the grout in between the mosaic pieces. Complete the grouting by scrubbing over the surface using a washing-up brush. Clean off any excess.

GARDEN CONSOLE

This console table was designed for a conventional indoor life, but has been given an outdoor paint treatment for a witty touch in the garden. It makes a useful extra surface for drinks or serving dishes when you are entertaining outside.

TOOLS AND MATERIALS

console table

medium-grade sandpaper

white acrylic wood primer

medium and fine paintbrushes

masonry paint

artist's acrylic paints in terracotta and pink

fine-textured masonry paint

acrylic scumble glaze

cloth

pencil

stencil cardboard

craft knife

stencil brush

polyurethane varnish

varnish brush

1 Prepare the table by sanding all the surfaces thoroughly. Prime with white acrylic wood primer and allow to dry. Tint some masonry paint with terracotta acrylic and use as a base coat. Allow to dry for 4–6 hours.

2 Tint some fine-textured masonry paint with pink acrylic, add scumble glaze and thin with water to the consistency of thick cream. Paint on and rub off with a cloth in the direction of the grain. Allow to dry.

3 Draw a leaf shape on a piece of stencil cardboard and cut out. Use terracotta paint to stencil a leaf on each corner of the table. Allow to dry, then varnish.

■ **OPPOSITE**
When the console table is not being used, you can have fun accessorizing it as if it were standing in a room indoors.

■ **RIGHT**
The essence of outdoor style is its simplicity. This garden store cupboard was built from nailed together pieces of driftwood.

PLANTS IN POTS: THE SOFT FURNISHINGS

Like vases of fresh flowers indoors, plants in containers provide strong accents of shape and colour in the garden, softening the lines of garden structures. They are prima donnas, flaunting their vivid colours while they are in their full glory, then bowing out to be replaced by the next star turn.

Decorative planting is one of the more pleasurable aspects of having an outdoor space. More than anything else, the choice of plants – and the containers they're planted in – will affect the mood of the garden and the finished look. Group containers by colour or create cameo gardens along a theme. Use an eclectic mix of containers or trim and shape shrubs and plants for a witty effect. Window boxes and hanging baskets will add special plant interest, bringing the colour to eye level for maximum impact.

■ ABOVE
There are no rules when it comes to arranging potted plants, and a witty and original choice of container will add something special.

■ OPPOSITE
Small fruit trees look lovely in pots, especially when covered in spring blossom.

DECORATIVE PLANTINGS

Once the basic framework of the garden is in place, the fun can start. Indoors, once you had painted the walls and laid the floors, you would be thinking of comfortable furniture, curtains and carpets. Outside, it is the planting that provides the soft furnishing. Without it, the garden would look very rigid and uninviting. Add a few plants, and immediately it takes on a much more comfortable feel. This is the part of gardening that is the most absorbing, even if you start off with no horticultural knowledge. A trip to the garden centre to browse among the seasonal plants becomes a treat.

Putting together the colours and textures to compose beautiful borders is one of the more pleasurable aspects of gardening, and is where your own creativity comes in. But soft furnishing in the context of the decorated garden is not just about borders. Decorative planting is about climbers that clamber curtain-like over arches and soften the outlines of vistas, and the hanging baskets that decorate walls. It is about the low-growing plants that create carpets of colour over what may previously have been uninspiring bare ground, and the plants that grow around and through established trees and shrubs, softening and beautifying their outlines. It is, finally, about feature planting in containers, positioned at focal points in the garden to create interest and impact.

■ OPPOSITE
A floral arbour makes a rich decorative frame for a piece of statuary, creating a theatrical effect. The roses, foxgloves and clematis make perfect stage curtains for this thoughtful stone "player".

■ BELOW
Trellis makes a permanent light screen across part of the garden, curtained in summer by the glossy green foliage and vivid flowers of a climbing rose.

■ ABOVE
The face of a cherub, in reflective mood, peers through the ivy, adding a charming touch to the eaves of a garden shed.

■ LEFT
Statuesque Greek pithoi are used here for architectural interest, rather than for planting. However, they have been softened and beautifully set off by stately euphorbias in vibrant shades of lime green.

WITTY WAYS WITH EVERYDAY PLANTS

Interesting gardens don't have to depend on a horticulturalist's expert knowledge of plants. Even the most ordinary plants can take on an exotic personality if pruned or planted in an original way. Many garden centres now sell ready-trained or standardized shrubs – you can add your own touch with a witty container, pretty underplanting or an attractive way of tying up the plants. There are no restrictions to the look you can create.

Topiary has come back into fashion, but this time it isn't restricted to large, formal gardens.

Box and privet grown in pots can be kept to a manageable size and still be clipped into architectural globes and conical shapes, as can any other plant which holds its shape well as it grows.

■ ABOVE
A standardized hydrangea grown in a pot makes an excellent patio plant. It has the appealing appearance of a miniature tree, and you can enjoy its flamboyant blooms without any worry that it might take over the garden.

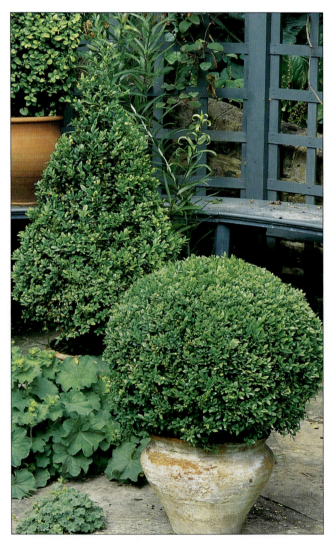

■ ABOVE
Small-scale topiary can be arranged, as here, in groups or used as boundary markers, down the edges of paths, between beds or to section off different parts of the garden.

■ ABOVE

As a change from allowing roses to scramble up walls or trellis, this one has been trained around a simple obelisk, the diagonally trailing stems adding greatly to its decorative appeal.

■ ABOVE

A potted chilli pepper plant would add a fun touch to any garden.

■ RIGHT

Fruit trees can be included in even the smallest gardens. Here, an espalier-trained apple is flanked by ballerina crab apples, which grow like poles.

HANGING GARDENS

An alternative to a conventional hanging basket is to design your planting so that the basket or container is made part of the display. Ordinary shopping baskets, buckets, agricultural containers, even kitchen equipment such as colanders, pots and pans with drainage holes drilled in the base, can all be used as hanging baskets with character.

If your chosen container is large and might possibly become too heavy when planted to be suspended, a useful trick is to put a layer of broken-up expanded polystyrene (left over from plant trays or the packaging around electrical goods) in the bottom of the container. This is lighter than the equivalent amount of compost (soil mix) and will provide good drainage for the plants.

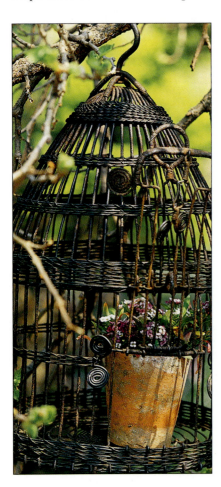

■ ABOVE
A witty interpretation of a hanging basket, this Indian birdcage makes an ideal receptacle for potted plants. Hung in a mulberry tree, it lends floral interest in early spring before the leaves have burst from their buds.

■ ABOVE
Free-standing, miniature mangers, stacked one over the other, make an unusual vertical feature in a tiny courtyard garden.

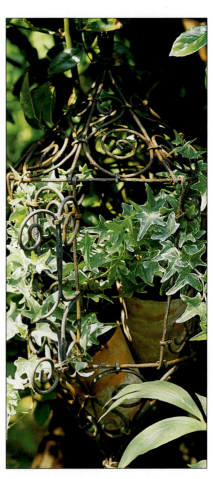

■ ABOVE
The most unlikely items can be used as hanging baskets. This pretty metal lantern from the Middle East has been filled with terracotta pots planted with variegated ivies to make a surprising and decorative hanging feature.

SUMMER BASKET

Hanging baskets are summer favourites in even the smallest gardens, bringing a floral splash – and fragrance if you choose appropriate plants – to walls, verandas, patios and even basement areas. Plant them early in the year, once the threat of late frosts has passed, to give the plants time to "get their toes in" and fill out.

TOOLS AND MATERIALS

hanging basket with chains or rope

coconut fibre liner

compost (soil mix)

trowel

water-retaining granules

slow-release fertilizer granules

6 variegated ivies

2 diascia

6 verbenas

watering can

1 Line the basket with the coconut fibre liner and part-fill with compost (soil mix), adding water-retaining and fertilizer granules as you go, according to the manufacturer's instructions.

2 Knock the ivy plants out of their pots and thread them through the sides of the basket. Place a diascia at either end of the basket. Add the verbenas.

■ BELOW
Verbena and diascia, with their trailing, wiry stems and pretty colouring, make an unrestrained combination that will quickly clothe this basket. The variegated ivy provides a foundation of foliage to offset the colours of the flowers.

3 Press more compost around each plant and down the sides of the basket so that everything is firmly bedded in. Water generously and hang the basket.

IDEAS FOR CONTAINERS

Almost any interesting receptacle will make a container for plants; in fact, the more unusual it is, the more impact it will create. Once you begin to see the potential in tins, boxes, baskets and jars, you'll be motivated to create really original plantings. Here are some ideas to get you started.

■ OPPOSITE
In China, glazed pots are frequently used as small ponds in courtyards. This pot contains a water lily, a flowering rush and an arum lily.

■ LEFT
With a couple of coats of varnish, an old wooden wine case will make an attractive and durable container for a miniature herb garden, which you could keep on the kitchen windowsill or near the back door, ready for use.

■ BELOW LEFT
Plant a kitchen garden in a selection of decorative oil cans, choosing a variety of sizes for a better show. These old cans have been planted with marjoram, nasturtiums, parsley, sage and borage.

■ BELOW
A flowerpot covered in mosaic makes an original container. This pot has been planted with miniature roses to match the flower motif design. A hole drilled into the base allows for drainage.

■ RIGHT
This large, sturdy cooking pot – found in a junk shop for next to nothing – makes a characterful container for plants.

POTTED HERB GARDEN

The use of time-honoured herbal remedies is enjoying renewed popularity as we come to appreciate the healing power of herbs. Here, herbs are planted in terracotta pots embellished with their botanical names and grouped together in a large saucer as a tribute to the apothecaries of old. Marigold, thyme, feverfew, lavender and rosemary have been used here, but you can plant whichever are your own favourites.

TOOLS AND MATERIALS

permanent marker pen

5 x 10cm/4in terracotta pots

selection of herbs: pot marigold (*Calendula*), thyme (*Thymus*), feverfew (*Matricaria*), lavender (*Lavandula*) and rosemary (*Rosmarinus*)

compost (soil mix) (optional)

terracotta saucer 36cm/14in in diameter

clay granules or gravel

1 Use the marker pen to write the botanical plants' names around the rims of the pots. Plant the herbs with additional compost (soil mix) if necessary.

2 Fill the saucer with clay granules or gravel and arrange the pots on top.

■ BELOW
Thyme, one of the useful herbs in this potted arrangement, can be drunk as a refreshing tisane to aid digestion.

HERBAL REMEDIES

Feverfew: a leaf rolled into a ball of bread can be taken for the symptoms of migraine
Lavender: the essential oil is known to be an effective treatment for minor burns
Pot marigold: a healing and mildly antiseptic herb
Rosemary: use in an infusion for scalp problems; makes an excellent hair rinse
Thyme: drunk as a tisane, purifying and disinfectant

BOUQUET GARNI DISPLAY

The classic bouquet garni consists of parsley, thyme and a bay leaf tied into a posy with string. It is used to impart flavour to stews, soups and sauces. In Provence, rosemary is always added as well. In all but the coldest areas, it is possible to gather these herbs fresh for most of the year. Here, the herbs have been planted in a small, moss-lined wooden crate, which would sit quite happily outdoors, on the kitchen windowsill. Planting containers along a theme in this way makes a delightful compromise between the useful and the decorative. Keep a small stock of the herbs to be dried for use mid-winter.

TOOLS AND MATERIALS

drill

wooden crate, 25 x 20 x 15cm/10 x 8 x 6in

40cm/16in sisal rope

permanent marker pen

paintbrush

liquid seaweed plant food

moss

small bay tree

thyme

2 parsley plants

compost (soil mix)

coarse grit

1 To make the handles, drill two holes in each end of the wooden crate. Thread the ends of a 20cm/8in length of rope through each of the holes from the outside and tie a knot in the ends to secure.

■ BELOW
The ingredients of the traditional bouquet garni will grow happily outside the kitchen window, within easy reach of the cook.

2 Use the permanent marker pen to write on each side of the crate. Paint the wood with an equal mixture of liquid seaweed plant food and water, to give it a weathered appearance.

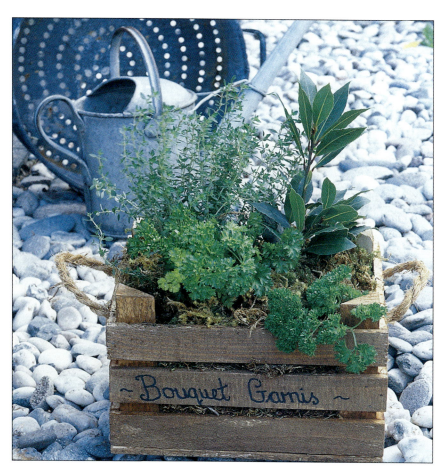

3 Line the crate with moss and plant the herbs in a mixture of three parts compost (soil mix) to one part coarse grit. Tuck more moss around the plants and water thoroughly.

TOPIARY HERBS

This is one of the most attractive and stylish ways to grow herbs, especially when they are planted in long-tom pots, which complete the sculptural effect. The herbs suitable for this treatment are those with woody stems such as rosemary, lemon verbena, santolina and lavender.

Select young plants with a strong, straight central stem, which can be trimmed to create the topiary shape. Once established, provided the herbs are regularly fed and watered and moved into larger pots as they grow, they should reach a good size and live for a number of years. A large plant trained like this would make a perfect centrepiece for a formal herb garden.

Bear in mind that the shape of long-tom pots makes them dry out more quickly than conventional pots, so frequent watering is essential. Prune the herbs every two weeks during the growing season. In colder areas, the plants will need winter protection, so pack them, pots and all, into a large wooden box filled with bark and stand them in a light, frost-free place.

■ OPPOSITE
To display a group of potted herbs to greatest effect, stand them against a plain background so that their shapes are clearly outlined.

TOOLS AND MATERIALS

scissors

young herb plants: rosemary, lavender, santolina or lemon verbena

long-tom pots

compost (soil mix)

coarse grit

washed gravel

1 Use the scissors to trim any side shoots from the central stem of each plant and to remove the foliage from the bottom half to two-thirds of the stem.

2 Trim the remaining foliage to shape. Transplant the herbs into terracotta pots using a mixture of two parts compost (soil mix) to one part coarse grit. Cover the compost with a layer of gravel. Water and stand in a sheltered, sunny position.

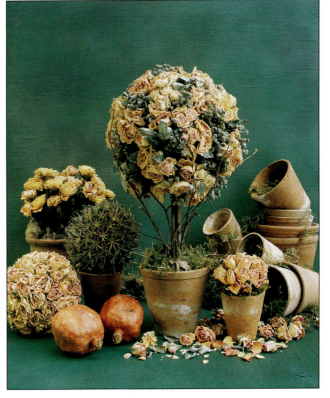

■ ABOVE
When the bloom of your summer roses has passed, cut the stems and stick into florist's foam for a topiary display.

ALPINE SHELL GARDEN

Create an alpine garden in a shell-decorated container for an unusual window box or garden decoration. The garden needs to be planted in spring after the frosts; once planted, it will need very little attention, producing masses of little flowers in summer in return for the occasional watering. It will rest in the winter, ready to grow with renewed vigour the following spring.

■ OPPOSITE
Choose alpine plants with small leaves and flowers to suit the miniature scale of this tiny garden-in-a-box.

TOOLS AND MATERIALS

wooden vegetable box

lime green emulsion (latex) paint

paintbrush

selection of about 8 alpine plants such as sempervivum, sedum and saxifrage

glue gun

12 scallop shells

large plastic bag

scissors

compost (soil mix)

selection of shells

1 Paint the box with lime green emulsion (latex) paint and let dry. This paint is really meant for indoor use, and will weather down in time to give softer tones. Water the plants thoroughly and allow to drain.

2 Using the glue gun, attach scallop shells all around the sides of the box. Line the box with plastic cut from a large bag, and make drainage holes in it using scissors.

3 Fill the box with a layer of compost (soil mix), then arrange the large shells on top.

4 Remove the plants from their pots and position them in the box. The roots can be wedged under a shell and bedded well into the compost.

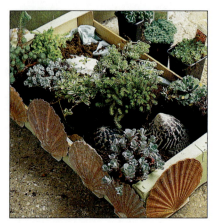

5 Water the box thoroughly. Until the plants grow to fill the box, you can add a few more small shells to cover the bare earth, if you like.

SEASHORE WINDOW BOX

As most window boxes are flat-fronted, they are easier to decorate than round pots. Here, the beautiful dark lustre of mussel shells left over from the dinner table lends impact to a co-ordinated planting of lavender and violas. Experiment with different shapes, using some of the shells face up and the others face down for a more varied effect.

TOOLS AND MATERIALS

mussel shells

small terracotta window box

glue gun

crocks or pebbles

compost (soil mix)

trowel

water-retaining granules

slow-release fertilizer granules

2 lavender plants

tray of violas

watering can

1 Arrange the mussel shells on the sides of the window box. When you are satisfied with your design, fix the shells in position using a glue gun. Leave until the glue has dried.

2 Place a layer of crocks or pebbles over the drainage holes inside the window box.

3 Partly fill the box with compost (soil mix), adding water-retaining and fertilizer granules as you go.

4 Plant the lavender at the back of the box. Press extra compost in front of the lavender until it is the right height for the violas. Plant the violas.

5 Top up with compost, firming it gently around the plants, and water generously.

■ OPPOSITE
The soft petals and subtle colour gradations of the violas make them the perfect match for the pearly interiors of the shells.

DECORATING POTS

Transforming an ordinary flower pot into something special really doesn't have to be difficult. There are so many media to choose from that it is an easy matter to find one that suits your decorative style. You may be happy with paint applied in bold geometric patterns or simple motifs. If you are skilled with a paintbrush, you might like to try something a little more figurative. Another easy option is to glue decorations on to your pots – ceramic chips, perhaps, to make a mosaic, or shells arranged in a simple textural pattern.

■ BELOW
This impressive garden urn is decorated with modern faces but has a look that is reminiscent of Byzantine icons. It will add a touch of grandeur to even the dullest corner of the garden or patio.

■ RIGHT
If you break a favourite plate or dish, this is a delightful way to continue to enjoy its colour and pattern. Use ceramic chips in co-ordinated colours and simple patterns to make striking mosaic pots.

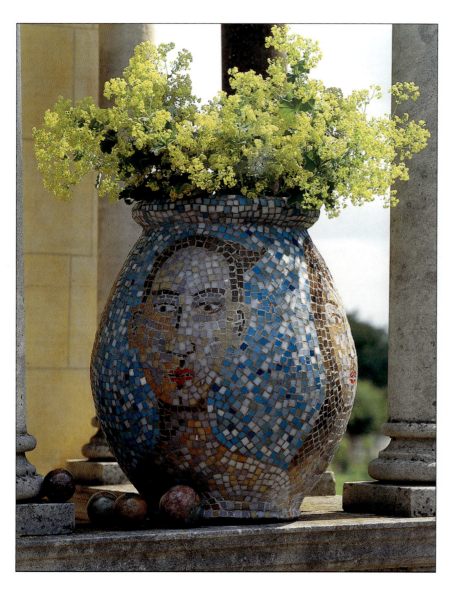

■ BELOW
This pot has been given a necklace of weathered glass "beads" dangling on wires from a wire ring fixed under the rim of the pot.

STENCILLED TERRACOTTA POT

Cheap terracotta pots can be made to look stylish and distinctive using simple stencilled designs. Choose paint colours that will enhance your plants and look good within your garden colour-scheme. Terracotta is porous and will absorb a lot of paint, so you may need several coats, depending on the colour you are using.

1 Measure the circumference of the pot at the top and bottom and divide into equal sections. Join each of these points with a vertical chalk line.

2 Mask off the outlines of the background shapes using masking tape and then paint. Add further coats as necessary and allow to dry.

■ BELOW
Once you have gained some confidence with simple stencils, experiment with freehand designs and other techniques such as sponging, stippling and dragging. Try other types of paint for different effects, such as metallic paints.

3 Tape the stencil to the pot and apply several coats of paint. Move the stencil around the rim of the pot and repeat to complete the design.

MEXICAN PAINTED POTS

Rings of folk-art motifs painted over stripes of vibrant colours give simple pots a rich Mexican look. This looks best if you leave some stripes of unpainted terracotta, and the style suits pots with fluted tops especially well. Stacked together and planted up with pelargoniums in hot summer colours, they make a lively garden feature.

TOOLS AND MATERIALS
....

terracotta pot with fluted top

masking tape

scissors

white undercoat

paintbrushes

gouache poster colours

semi-gloss polyurethane varnish

varnish brush

1 Mark the stripes on the pot using masking tape. Cut some lengths into narrower widths to give variations in the finished design. Bear in mind that the areas covered with masking tape will remain natural terracotta.

2 Paint the main body of the pot, below the rim, with white undercoat. When dry, paint in the coloured stripes, changing the colour for each band. Leave to dry.

3 When the paint is completely dry, carefully peel off the masking tape.

4 Using a fine brush and the white undercoat, paint a series of traditional motifs along the stripes. When completely dry, coat with varnish.

■ OPPOSITE
The hot colours of these painted pots will hold their own in the sunniest spot on the patio. Fill them with vividly coloured flowering plants or exotic-looking succulents.

PAINTING A BORAGE BUCKET

There is an old country saying that "a garden without borage is a garden without courage", which refers to the old herbalists' belief that this plant has the ability to lift the spirits. In addition to its medicinal properties – its oil is as potent as that of evening primrose – its pretty, blue, cucumber-scented flowers will gladden the heart when added to a glass of summer punch or used to decorate a salad.

■ OPPOSITE
Beautiful blue borage flowers look great against the silvery grey of a galvanized bucket. Here, they pick up the blue stencilled design on the watering can.

TOOLS AND MATERIALS

pencil

stencil cardboard

craft knife

cutting mat

masking tape

galvanized bucket, 18cm/7in in diameter

artist's acrylic paints in mid-blue, deep blue and white

stencil brush

fine paintbrush

polyurethane varnish

varnish brush

borage plants

1 Draw two or three borage flowers on a piece of stencil cardboard and cut out the outlines with a craft knife to make a stencil. Attach the stencil to the side of the bucket, using masking tape, and paint the flowers in mid-blue in an overlapping random pattern.

2 Using a fine paintbrush, add details to the flowers in deep blue and white. Protect the decoration with a coat of polyurethane varnish and let it dry before adding the borage plants.

■ RIGHT
The borage plant motif can make even the most practical of gardening equipment look charming. Adapt the idea for other pieces, perhaps painting them with other simple flowers such as daisies or pansies.

VERDIGRIS BUCKET

There is something irresistible about the luminous, subtle blue-green tones of verdigris. It is a colour that always complements plants and it is not difficult to reproduce on an ordinary galvanized bucket. Alternatively, you can use the same painting technique, substituting rust-coloured acrylic for aqua, to produce a rusted effect.

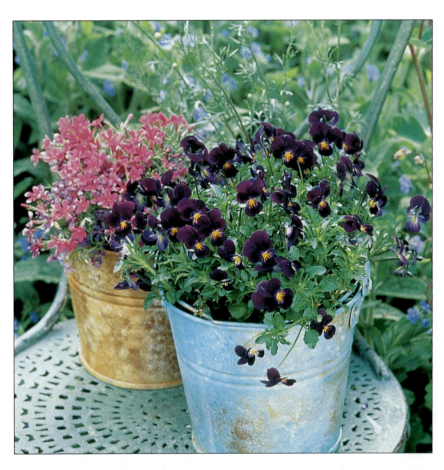

TOOLS AND MATERIALS

medium-grade sandpaper

galvanized bucket

metal primer

paintbrushes

gold emulsion (latex) paint

amber shellac

artist's acrylic paint in white and aqua-green

natural sponge

polyurethane varnish

varnish brush

■ LEFT
The pale, cool aqua tone of verdigris makes a wonderful foil for these delicate and velvety dark violas.

1 Sand the bucket, then prime with metal primer and allow to dry. Paint with gold paint and leave the bucket to dry for at least 2–3 hours.

2 Paint the bucket with amber shellac and let dry. Mix white acrylic with aqua-green to make the verdigris, and thin it to a watery consistency.

3 Sponge the verdigris paint over the shellac and allow to dry for 1–2 hours before applying a coat of varnish.

LEAD CHIMNEY

Lead has been used to make garden containers for centuries, and its chalky blue-grey tones look wonderful with plants. But lead is incredibly heavy and very expensive, so here is a way of faking it, using a plastic chimney and a simple paint effect.

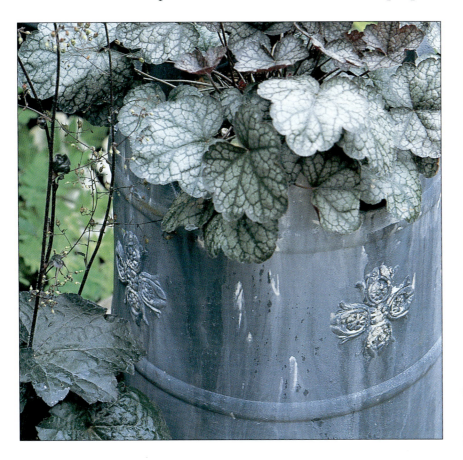

■ LEFT
A lead-coloured container looks stunning filled with silvery foliage and pale flowers.

1 Sand the chimney to give a key for the paint. Paint with one coat of acrylic primer and leave to dry for 1–2 hours.

2 Apply a coat of charcoal grey emulsion (latex) and leave to dry for 2–3 hours.

3 Tint some scumble glaze with white emulsion and thin with water. Paint over the chimney randomly using a large artist's paintbrush. Blend the colour by washing over the surface with a wet brush and leave to dry.

4 Add more of the white scumble mixture to parts of the chimney to "age" the surface. Leave to dry, then paint with a coat of polyurethane varnish.

TIN-CAN PLANT NURSERY

Seedlings can be decorative in themselves, so pick them out from their seed trays into a collection of tin cans mounted on a wall plaque. They can grow on there, sheltered by the wall and high above any threatening late frosts, until they are ready to be planted out. The plaque itself looks wonderful made from ordinary tinned steel cans, but if you want to add a bit more colour, scour delicatessens for vividly printed cans.

■ OPPOSITE
Printed and plain tin cans take on a new and more interesting appearance when they are massed together on a Mediterranean blue wall panel.

TOOLS AND MATERIALS

wooden board about 60 x 30cm/24 x 12in

undercoat

paintbrush

blue gloss paint

variety of empty cans with paper labels removed

can opener

tin snips

pliers

hammer

nail

tacks

1 Paint the board with a coat of undercoat and one or two coats of gloss paint, allowing each coat to dry before applying the next.

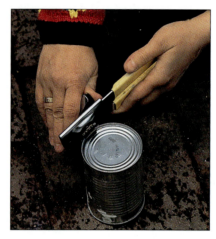

2 Stand the cans open end down and, using the can opener, cut round half of the bottom.

3 Using tin snips, cut open the side of the can to make two equal flaps.

4 Open out the sides with pliers and snip a V-shape into each one. Bend up the can bottom in line with the sides. Pierce the bottom of each can by hammering a nail through it.

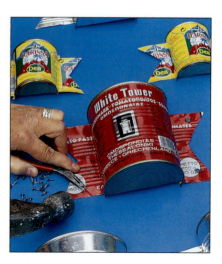

5 Arrange all the cans on the board, then tack them in place, hammering a tack through each point of the side flaps.

MOSS AND NETTING URN

This rustic urn is created from nothing more remarkable than chicken wire and moss: a collection of these elegant containers would make wonderful garden decorations for a special occasion, flanking steps or ranged along a balustrade. Even without the moss filling, the wire shape makes a quirky sculpture in itself. When the urns are not in use, they will keep their colour longer if they are kept in a dark place, as moss fades quite quickly in daylight.

TOOLS AND MATERIALS
....

wire cutters

chicken wire

moss

florist's wire

20cm/8in plastic pot

1 Cut a 1.5m/1½yd length of chicken wire. Fold it in half so that the raw edges meet and pack a layer of moss between the layers of wire.

2 Fold the chicken wire and moss "sandwich" in half lengthways and join the edges securely together with lengths of florist's wire.

3 Slip the plastic pot into the top end of the tube (the end with no rough edges) and form the lip of the urn by folding the chicken wire outwards from the rim of the pot.

4 Leaving the pot in place, firmly squeeze the chicken wire with both hands just below the pot to make the stem of the urn.

5 Make the base by folding the rough edges in and squeezing and squashing the wire into the desired shape. Stand the urn up periodically while you do this to check that it is level.

■ **RIGHT**
Whether the moss is fresh or has been allowed to dry out, the container has a pleasingly textural quality.

EARTHY PAINTED POTS

Liquid seaweed plant food is a wonderful rich brown colour and can be diluted and painted on to terracotta pots to encourage the growth of moss and give the appearance of age. Undiluted, the colour is very deep and looks beautiful as a decoration for terracotta. You can either preserve this rich colour with a coat of varnish or you could leave the pots unsealed: most of the coating will be worn away by the weather if the pots are left outside, leaving soft faded patterns, like traces of ancient frescoes.

1 Use masking tape to protect the areas of the pot that you want to remain unpainted. Brush liquid seaweed plant food on to the unmasked areas and leave to dry completely.

2 Peel off the masking tape and seal the whole pot with a coat of matt varnish, if you wish to retain the rich brown colour.

■ ABOVE
Beautiful pots in rich natural hues of terracotta and earthy dark brown hold a winter arrangement of twigs and cones.

CHICKEN BOX PLANT STAND

It is fun, especially in spring when the plants are low, to hoist a few flowers on high. And here is a witty way to achieve that: make a decorative wooden chicken nesting on a box, raise it on a stake and fill the box with pots of seasonal flowers.

■ OPPOSITE
Use this bright wooden chicken to bring a splash of instant colour to any part of the garden that needs perking up for a week or two as the seasons change.

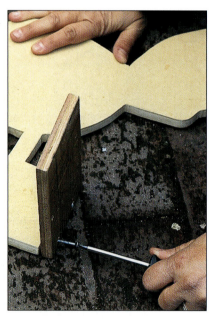

TOOLS AND MATERIALS

pencil

paper

tape measure

scissors

MDF (medium density fiberboard), 60 x 60cm/2 x 2ft

jigsaw

25mm/1in plywood, at least 75 x 45cm/30 x 18in

6 screws

screwdriver

undercoat

paintbrushes

enamel paint in red, orange, white, blue, black and green

7.5 x 5cm/3 x 2in post, about 120cm/4ft long

1 Draw the chicken shape on paper, with a box back for it to stand on measuring 17 x 9cm/6½ x 3½in. Cut out the template and transfer the design to the MDF. Cut out using a jigsaw. Cut three pieces of plywood 17 x 9cm/6½ x 3½in and one piece 17 x 5cm/6½ x 2in.

2 Screw the two larger plywood panels to the chicken, one on either side. Screw the narrower panel between them, 3cm/1in from the bottom edge of the side panels, to make the base. Screw the final plywood panel onto the front.

3 Paint both sides of the chicken and the box with a layer of undercoat and allow to dry.

4 Sketch the chicken's features on both sides of the chicken shape and paint with enamel paints. Paint the box green. Allow to dry overnight.

5 Screw the post to the back of the box to allow it to stand upright.

GARDEN DECORATIONS AND ACCESSORIES

Now comes the icing on the cake and the finishing touch: when your garden is looking a picture and you want to enhance its design and its planting, add some well-judged artefacts to draw the eye or raise a smile for a truly decorated garden.

Decorating your outdoor room is enormous fun. Allow yourself to be idiosyncratic in your choice of embellishments. Mosaic spheres, china tiles or a mosaic clock could make unusual and original garden features. Mobiles and wind chimes look delightful and produce gentle sounds to soothe the ear, while a customized birdhouse will attract bird life to your garden and help to support the birds through the winter months. If you're looking to add romance to your garden, hang a few decorative hearts here and there.

■ ABOVE
Galvanized metal artefacts work best dotted casually about the garden.

■ OPPOSITE
Whether it is fruit, vegetables or seedlings you want to protect, make a scarecrow to double as an amusing garden sculpture. This dapper chap with a colander face wears a denim jacket and a sporty panama hat.

OUTDOOR DECORATIONS

Sculpture is the classic outdoor art form, but if you don't have money to spend on garden decorations or if the space in your garden is limited, then there are plenty of alternatives. You can use anything that adds structure and form to the garden.

Large plant pots and boxes are decorative as well as functional. The traditional example is the classic urn, but you don't even have to go that far. Ordinary pots, painted or carefully arranged in groups, can make a statement, as can novel containers. Think of some unusual hanging baskets, such as colanders, baskets or buckets, or gather potted plants into a spectacular container, such as an old wheelbarrow, to make a display. You can add more purely decorative ideas, such as whirligigs, wind chimes, driftwood or pebble collections. Or you can fashion your own decorations – motifs such as hearts or stars made from twigs and branches, wire or raffia.

■ OPPOSITE

An old wicker mannequin teamed with a miniature wirework version makes an amusing and unexpected decoration.

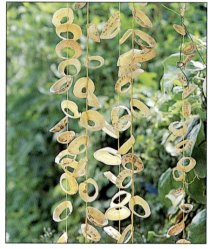

■ ABOVE

A collection of limpet shell rings hung on strong threads makes an attractive, joyous wind chime.

■ ABOVE

This inexpensive, painted bamboo birdcage, filled with potted pinks, makes a charming ornament.

■ LEFT

Even simple galvanized shapes take on decorative appeal: all they need is a couple of coats of paint.

DECORATIVE MOSAIC SPHERES

Mosaic spheres inspired by millefiori African beadwork would make unusual garden decorations. Based on wooden or polystyrene balls, they can be decorated with broken china, glass mosaic tiles or fragments of mirror. If you use a polystyrene foundation, the spheres will be quite light and could be hung in a tree.

■ BELOW
Mosaic stars dotted amongst the foliage can add an element of surprise to a blooming hedge of roses.

TOOLS AND MATERIALS

polystyrene or wooden spheres

PVA (white) glue

paintbrush

pencil

selection of old china

mirror

tile nippers

rubber gloves

waterproof tile adhesive

powdered waterproof tile grout

vinyl matt emulsion (latex) or acrylic paint

nailbrush

soft cloth

1 Seal the polystyrene or wooden spheres with diluted PVA (white) glue. Leave to dry.

2 Using a pencil, draw a simple design on a sphere. A combination of circular shapes works well, but experiment with other geometric shapes and abstract designs.

3 Cut the china and mirror into different sized pieces using tile nippers. Stick the pieces to the sphere using waterproof tile adhesive. Leave overnight to dry.

■ RIGHT
Position the spheres to suggest bowls mid-game for a fun and very modern ornamental display.

4 Mix powdered grout with water and use a little vinyl matt emulsion (latex) or acrylic paint to colour it. Wearing rubber gloves, rub the grout into the surface of the sphere, filling all the cracks between the tesserae.

5 Leave for a few minutes until the surface has dried, then brush off excess grout using a stiff nailbrush.

6 Leave to dry overnight, then polish with a soft dry cloth.

CHINA TILES

If you want to use mosaic as a garden decoration but are daunted by a large-scale project, you could try making some of these small one-off tiles. Try out simple patterns, using a selection of broken china, and think of the tiles as sketches or experiments before embarking on more complex mosaics.

■ OPPOSITE
These mosaic tiles could be displayed singly or in groups, stuck on a garden wall or used to decorate a table.

TOOLS AND MATERIALS
....

plain white tiles

PVA (white) glue

paintbrush

pencil

selection of old china

tile nippers

tile adhesive

acrylic paint or cement dye

powdered waterproof tile grout

rubber gloves

nailbrush

soft cloth

1 Prime the back of a plain tile with diluted PVA (white) glue and leave to dry. Draw a simple design on the back of the tile using a pencil.

2 Cut a selection of china into small pieces that will fit into your design, using tile nippers. Arrange the tesserae in groups according to colour and shape.

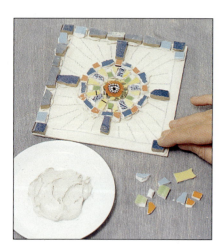

3 Dip the tesserae into tile adhesive and press them, one by one, on to the tile, using the drawing as a guide. When the tile is completely covered, leave it to dry overnight.

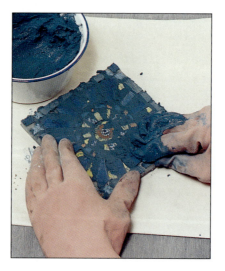

4 Mix acrylic paint or cement dye with powdered waterproof tile grout. Add a little water and mix to a dough-like consistency. Wearing rubber gloves, rub the grout into the surface of the mosaic, making sure that all the gaps are filled. Leave to dry for about ten minutes.

5 Scrub the surface of the tile with a stiff nailbrush to remove all the excess grout, then leave the tile to dry for 24 hours. Polish the surface with a soft dry cloth.

MOSAIC CLOCK

This clockface is decorated with mosaic made from hand-painted Mexican tiles. While the painting on the tiles is very free, and they have been cut into uneven shapes, the resulting tesserae are used to construct a precise geometric design that draws attention to the positions of the hands, making it easy to read the time. The base of the clock is made from two pieces of wood, with a hole cut into the thick piece at the back to accommodate the clock mechanism and batteries. The clock can live outdoors, but position it in a sheltered place, where it will receive the maximum amount of protection from the weather.

TOOLS AND MATERIALS

4mm/⅛in plywood

2cm/¾in chipboard

compasses

marker pen or pencil

ruler

jigsaw

drill and bits

clock movement and hands

PVA (white) glue

paintbrush

strong wood glue

4 clamps or heavy weights

tile nippers

selection of plain and patterned tiles

cement-based tile adhesive

shells

flexible (putty) knife

rubber gloves

sponge

sandpaper

soft cloth

1 Draw a 40cm/16in circle on both the plywood and the chipboard, and cut out with the jigsaw . Drill a hole through the centre of the chipboard circle large enough to take the jigsaw blade. Saw a hole to accommodate the clock mechanism and batteries. Drill a hole through the centre of the plywood circle for the spindle. Prime both pieces with diluted PVA (white) glue and let dry.

2 Stick the plywood and chipboard circles together using strong wood glue. Clamp the pieces together or leave under heavy weights overnight to dry.

3 Draw a circle in the centre of the plywood circle with a radius of the length of the minute hand. Using a marker pen or pencil, divide the face into quarters and use these as the basis for your design.

4 Using tile nippers, cut the patterned tiles into small irregular shapes. This design uses tiles in three different patterns, to differentiate the areas of the clockface. Stick the tiles on with cement-based tile adhesive, making sure they lie flat.

5 Cut plain tiles into small rectangular shapes for the rim of the clock. Tile the border, marking the positions of the quarter hours. When attaching the shells, make sure they are positioned so that they will not obstruct the movement of the clock hands.

6 Use a flexible (putty) knife to smooth tile adhesive around the rim of the clock. Wearing rubber gloves, work the adhesive over the clockface, making sure all the gaps are filled. Wipe clean with a sponge and leave to dry for approximately 24 hours.

7 Sand off any excess cement and polish with a soft dry cloth.

8 Attach the clock, fitting the movement and batteries into the hole at the back. Insert the spindle through the central hole and fit the hands.

■ RIGHT
Simple groups of pretty shells have been used to mark the quarter hours on this clockface.

CUSTOMIZED NESTING BOX

Ready-made nesting boxes are available in every shape and size, but a simple box can be transformed with a lick of paint and a few decorative touches. This house is painted in Shaker style and finished with a finial cut from scrap timber and an apple twig for a perch. To ensure that a nesting box gives you maximum pleasure, position it so that you will be able to see it from a window when you are indoors as well as when you are out in the garden.

TOOLS AND MATERIALS

nesting box

vinyl matt emulsion (latex) paint in 2 colours

paintbrush

marker pen

decorative finial

PVA (white) glue

drill

apple twig

1 Paint the box with emulsion (latex) paint in the first colour and leave to dry. Draw the door shape and the heart motifs using a marker pen.

2 Fill in the design and paint the finial with the second colour of emulsion paint and leave to dry completely.

3 Glue the finial in place at the front of the roof ridge using PVA (white) glue. Drill a hole to fit the apple twig beneath the entrance hole. Apply glue to the twig and push it into position.

■ OPPOSITE
Hang this pretty nesting box where the birds will be safe from predators; they will be happier if there is some overhanging foliage to give them a little shelter and privacy.

■ LEFT
If your birds would prefer a more metropolitan dwelling, paint a ready-made nesting box blue-grey and roof it with copper foil. The door surround is also made from copper foil – bend this back on itself, not into the hole, so that there are no sharp edges around the entrance to the box.

HANGING BIRD-FEEDING TABLE

If you put out food and fresh water regularly, your garden will soon become a haven for wild birds. The birds quickly get to know and will pass the word around to make your bird-feeding table a popular stopping-off point.

There is immense pleasure to be gained from watching the different species that come to feed daily. This bird-feeding table is made from rough timber, with a lip around the edge to stop nuts and seeds rolling off.

TOOLS AND MATERIALS

2 lengths of rough timber, 25 x 12.5 x 1cm/10 x 5½ x ½in

2 battens 25 x 2.5 x 2.5cm/ 10 x 1 x 1in

nails

hammer

4 battens 28 x 5 x 1cm/ 11 x 2 x ½in

wood preservative

small decorator's paintbrush

pencil

ruler

4 brass hooks

scissors

2m/6½ft sisal string

1 To make the base of the table, lay the two lengths of rough timber side by side and place the 25cm/10in battens across the wood, one at each end. Nail the battens securely in place.

2 Nail the four 28cm/11in battens around the edges of the base, allowing a lip of at least 2.5cm/1in. Paint all the surfaces of the table with wood preservative and leave to dry.

3 Use a pencil and ruler to mark a point in each corner of the table. Screw in a brass hook on each of the points.

4 Cut the sisal string into four equal lengths and tie a small loop in one end of each piece. Attach each loop to a hook, then gather up the strings above the table and tie in a loop for hanging.

■ OPPOSITE
String is tied to a hook in each corner so that the table can be hung in a tree, out of reach of predators.

■ LEFT
Specialist bird seed suppliers can provide information about which types of seed will attract which particular species of bird.

COPPER BIRDBATH

You will have endless pleasure watching the birds preening and cleaning in this beautiful, yet eminently practical, beaten copper birdbath. Maintain a constant supply of fresh drinking water all year round to ensure the health and happiness of the birds in your locality.

1 Using a chinagraph pencil and a piece of looped string, mark a 45cm/18in circle on the copper sheet.

2 Wearing protective gloves, cut out the circle with a pair of tin snips. Smooth the sharp edge using a file.

3 Lay the copper circle on a blanket and lightly hammer it from the centre. Spread the dips out to the rim. Repeat, starting in the centre each time, until you have the required shape. To make the perch, loop 1m/39in copper wire and hold the ends in a vice. Fasten a hook into the chuck of a drill. Put the hook through the loop and run the drill to twist the wire. Drill three holes, equally spaced, around the rim of the bath. Divide the remaining wire into three equal lengths and knot one end of each. Thread through the holes from beneath the bath. Slip the twisted wire over two straight wires to form a perch, and bend the tops of the wires together into a loop for hanging.

TOOLS AND MATERIALS

chinagraph pencil

string

9mm/⅜in 20 SWG copper sheet

protective gloves

tin snips

file

blanket

hammer

4m/13ft medium copper wire

bench vice

strong hook

slow-speed electric drill

3mm/⅛in bit

■ ABOVE
This elegant birdbath, with spare, modern lines, features a wire perch suspended over the water for the birds to stand on as they drink.

GAZEBO FEEDER

Constructed from a small glass lantern and some recycled tin cans, this little bird-feeder will hang like a jewel amongst the foliage of a tree.

TOOLS AND MATERIALS

glass lantern

tape measure

thin glass

chinagraph pencil

try-square

glass cutter

ruler

protective gloves

shiny tin can, washed and dried

tin snips

flux and soldering iron

solder

try-square

fine wire mesh

1 This lantern required extra glass to be installed. If this is the case with yours, measure the areas required and reduce all measurements by 6mm/¼in to allow for the metal border. Using a chinagraph pencil, mark the measurements on the glass, then cut out by running a glass cutter in a single pass along a ruler. Wearing protective gloves, tap along the line to break the glass. Cut 9mm/⅜in strips of metal from a tin can using tin snips.

2 Wrap a strip of metal around each edge of each glass panel. Trim, then smear soldering flux on to the mating surfaces of each corner. Solder the corner joints of each panel. Heat a joint with a soldering iron and apply the solder. Remove the iron to allow the solder to cool and set.

■ BELOW
This sophisticated bird-feeder makes a delightful detail in a quiet garden corner.

3 Measure the openings for the hoppers and fold sections of the tin can to suit, using a try-square or ruler to keep the fold lines straight. Solder the meeting points of each hopper. Cut out a platform from fine wire mesh and solder the platform, the panels and the hoppers in place on the framework.

GILDED POTS

Ordinary terracotta pots, gilded and filled with candle wax, make beautiful, sparkling garden lights. Use pots in a range of sizes and group them on tables, patios, walls and outdoor shelves for a magical effect in the soft evening light.

■ OPPOSITE
Fabulous golden pots glitter in the candle flames for a simple supper or an evening party in the garden.

TOOLS AND MATERIALS

assorted terracotta pots

self-hardening clay

red oxide primer

paintbrushes

water-based gold size

Dutch metal leaf in gold

soft cloth or soft-bristled brush

amber shellac

artist's acrylic paint in white and aqua

scissors

wick

wooden skewers

candle wax

double boiler

1 Plug the drainage hole of each pot with a little clay and leave to set. Prime the pots with red oxide primer and leave for 3–4 hours to dry.

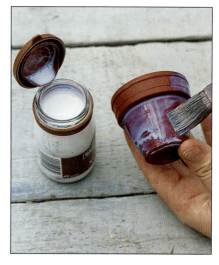

2 Apply a coat of water-based gold size and allow to dry for about 30 minutes, or until the size is transparent and tacky.

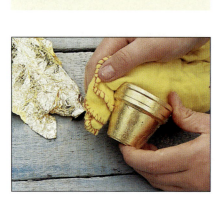

3 To apply the Dutch metal leaf, lift the sheets carefully and lay them on the size, gently smoothing each one with a cloth or soft-bristled brush. Brush off any excess leaf and polish gently with a soft cloth.

4 Apply a coat of amber shellac to seal the metal leaf and leave for at least 30 minutes until completely dry.

5 To age the pots, tint a little white acrylic with aqua and thin with water. Brush on the paint and rub off with a cloth. Leave to dry. Suspend a length of wick in each pot by tying it to a skewer laid across the top and check that it reaches the bottom. Melt the wax in a double boiler and pour it into the pot. Leave to set overnight.

IRON LANTERN

Give a new aluminium lantern the more appealing appearance of aged iron. Even the simplest shapes and brashest finishes become infinitely more pleasing when given the well-worn look of a lantern of yore.

1 Stick masking tape over all the glass of the lantern. Sand the metal to provide a key. Paint all the metal parts of the lantern with a coat of metal primer. Allow to dry for 2–3 hours, then paint on a silver base coat.

2 Dip the natural sponge into black emulsion (latex) and dab on to the lantern. Allow to dry for 1–2 hours.

■ BELOW
Subtle and darkly interesting, this lantern gains an antique quality once it has been painted.

3 Mix red oxide acrylic paint with a little water and, using an artist's paintbrush, drip this down the lantern to resemble rust. Spray with a water spray. Allow to dry for 1–2 hours. Varnish, leave to dry, then remove the tape.

GLASS JAR NIGHT-LIGHT

When lit with a small candle, this stained-glass night-light throws patches of coloured light on to the surrounding foliage. One jar is used as the base and another is broken into small fragments that are painted with glass paints. The fragments are then stuck on to the base jar and the gaps grouted. If your jars are not the same size, use the smaller one as the base.

TOOLS AND MATERIALS

2 glass jars

old dish towel

goggles

protective gloves

hammer

scrap paper

newspaper

reusable adhesive

glass paints

paintbrushes

solvent-free, rapid setting
epoxy resin glue

white cellulose filler

grout spreader

scourer

sandpaper

acrylic paint

1 Wrap a jar in a dish towel. Wearing goggles and gloves, and covering your hair, smash the jar with a hammer. Place the pieces to be used as tesserae on scrap paper with the sharp edges facing downwards to avoid cutting yourself. Wrap the unused glass in newspaper and dispose of it carefully.

2 Use reusable adhesive to pick up the broken pieces of glass and turn them over so that the sharp edges face upwards. Paint the concave surface of each fragment with glass paint in different colours. Leave to dry. Glue the painted fragments to the base jar using solvent-free epoxy resin glue. Leave until completely dry.

3 Spread cellulose filler over the surface, smoothing it into the top and bottom edges of the jar, and wiping off any excess. Let dry. If any cracks appear as it dries, smooth over more filler. When dry, clean off excess filler with a scourer and water, and sandpaper. Paint over the filler with acrylic paint.

■ RIGHT
This delightful lantern gives a subtle glow in the garden at night, looking like a miniature stained-glass window.

TWIGWAM

Plant supports are functional, but that doesn't mean they can't be decorative too. This one, made from branches pruned from garden trees interwoven with willow, makes a charming structural detail in a flower bed. Alternatively, it can be used to support clematis or any other climber for a wonderful, free-standing, outdoor floral display.

TOOLS AND MATERIALS

3 unbranched poles, about 90cm/3ft long

string or strands of willow

3 unbranched poles, about 30cm/12in long

plenty of fine, freshly cut willow branches

1 Stand up the three taller poles to form a "wigwam" and tie them together at the top with string or willow.

2 Stand the three shorter poles between the longer ones and tie them in the same way. Start to weave the willow branches in and out of the poles, working upwards from the bottom.

3 Once enough of the wigwam has been woven to keep the shorter poles securely in position, untie them. Continue weaving until the shorter poles are almost covered.

■ RIGHT
This woven willow support would look pretty entwined with sweet peas or nasturtiums, to give instant height in a summer border.

CHICKEN WIRE CLOCHE

This quirky chicken wire cloche can be used to protect plants from slugs and birds or can be simply "planted" into the flowerbed as a charming and original miniature obelisk.

TOOLS AND MATERIALS

wire cutters

fine-mesh chicken wire

pliers

medium-gauge garden wire

2 Use the pliers to squeeze the wire into shape. At the top, squeeze each lozenge shape as tightly as it will go. Continue to pinch the wires together down the tube, squeezing each hole less and less until you reach the fullest part of the shape.

1 Using wire cutters, cut a piece of chicken wire about 50 x 50cm/20 x 20in. Roll it to form a tube, making sure the twisted sides of each lozenge shape run vertically. Join the tube by twisting the cut ends of the wire securely in place around each other.

3 At the bottom of the cloche, make a "skirt" by narrowing the shape again, then letting it fan out gracefully. Wind garden wire tightly around the top to finish the cloche.

■ RIGHT
With a bit of original thought, you can turn an everyday material like chicken wire into an amusing miniature folly for the garden.

85

WIND CHIMES

A walk on the beach or in the woods to gather weathered driftwood and twigs, and a forage in the potting shed, will provide you with all the materials you need to make these rustic wind chimes. The bells are made from miniature terracotta pots with metal vine-eyes as clappers. Provided the pots have no cracks, the wind chimes will sound like distant cow-bells, adding the extra dimension of gentle sounds to the sensual delights of your garden.

TOOLS AND MATERIALS

wire cutters

galvanized wire

drill and bit

3 corks

4 weathered twigs of different sizes, the largest 30cm/12in long

2 metal vine-eyes

2 miniature terracotta pots

1 Cut one 50cm/20in and two 30cm/12in lengths of wire. Drill a hole through the centre of each cork. Make a hanging loop at one end of the longer piece of wire. Just beneath the loop, twist the wire around the centre of the longest twig and thread on a cork.

2 Add the next twig, either twisting the wire around it as before, or drilling a hole and threading it on. Add a second cork, followed by the third twig and the third cork. Make a hook in the end of the remaining wire, trimming it if necessary. Drill a hole through one end of the final twig and hook it on to the wire.

3 Thread a vine-eye on to each of the shorter lengths of wire and bend over 2.5cm/1in of the wire so that it lies flat against the vine-eye. Wrap the long end of the wire around the vine-eye in a spiral. Thread each vine-eye through the drainage hole in one of the terracotta pots, so that the wide end of the vine-eye becomes the clapper and the narrow end protrudes from the pot.

4 Hang up the wind chimes and attach the bells, making sure that the wind chimes balance. Twist the wires protruding from the bells securely around the twig.

■ OPPOSITE
Wind chimes made with natural materials found in the garden blend effortlessly into its decorative scheme.

■ RIGHT
The charm of this alternative wind chime lies in its simplicity. Sand dollars provide the form, while the cockle shells strung onto raffia provide the music.

SEAWORN SHELL MOBILE

Spend a day on the beach hunting among the rocks and pebbles and you are bound to come across plenty of materials for this delicate mobile. Limpet shells worn by the sea and sand often develop central holes, which makes them perfect for stringing. The stone-effect beads used here come in a range of smooth shapes and natural colours. Real pebbles that have weathered holes in them could also be used, but they might be too heavy to allow the mobile to move in the breeze.

1 Drill a hole through both ends of two pieces of driftwood, each about 36cm/14in long. Cut two 56cm/22in lengths of string and knot a bead 3cm/1in from the end of each. Thread one end of each piece of string through the hole in the driftwood for the top of the frame, and secure with a knot. Thread the other end through the hole in the bottom piece of wood. Thread a small, drilled cockle shell on to the end of each piece of string and secure with a knot.

2 To make the limpet wind chime, drill six holes, about 2cm/¾in apart, along a small piece of driftwood. Cut six 38cm/15in lengths of rough string. Thread and tie the limpet shells on to the strings and thread through the holes in the driftwood. Secure with knots and cut off any excess string.

3 For the tailed winkle (periwinkle) shell, cut some short lengths of raffia and glue four or five into the mouth of each conch shell, using epoxy resin glue. Leave to dry. Drill a hole in the top of the large winkle shell.

4 Make a plait with three long strands of raffia, bind one end with tape and thread it through the hole in the winkle shell. Tie a knot in the end of the plait and pull it inside the shell. Tie beads and small pieces of driftwood on to the plait.

5 Gather together the conch shells and glue the ends of their raffia tails inside the mouth of the winkle shell, so that the shells hang down like a tail.

6 To assemble the mobile, drill two holes in the top of the frame. Thread the raffia plait through one of the holes and knot at the top. Tie a doubled length of string to each end of the top of the wind chime. Tie both strings around a large, round bead, then thread the ends through the second hole in the top of the frame and secure with a knot.

■ **ABOVE**
Hang the shell mobile where it will catch the breeze and its gentle tinkling will remind you of days at the seaside.

HEARTS IN THE GARDEN

Hearts hold universal appeal, and there is no reason why they shouldn't find a home in the garden. You will be surprised by what you can make from the most rudimentary weather-proof materials. Garden wire, chicken wire, twigs and raffia are all ideal. The beauty of the heart shape is that it is very easy to achieve. Just start with a circle of wire and bend it into a dip at one side and a point at the other. Twigs can be coaxed into curves to make the two halves of a heart, then bound together at the top and bottom.

■ ABOVE
A simple chicken wire heart decorated and suspended with paper string makes a pretty decoration for a shed door or the bare side of a wall in a sheltered spot.

■ ABOVE
This heart-shaped wreath carries a seasonal message. The twig framework is wound with variegated ivy and red berries, with a Christmas rose to finish.

■ ABOVE
A heart made from garden wire is knotted all around with sturdy bundles of natural raffia dyed green and ochre.

■ LEFT
Few things can be more romantic than a lavender heart. Make this with fresh lavender bound on to a wire frame, then let it dry naturally.

WIRE HEART

This delightful filigree heart is not difficult to make from ordinary garden wire, and it is certainly robust enough to withstand a winter outside. It is composed of small hearts bent into shape with pliers, then wired together in a beautiful overall design. Make one to hang in a tree, or make several in different sizes, so that they take on a sculptural quality. This one, flanked on all sides by neatly trimmed trees, is given throne-like importance.

TOOLS AND MATERIALS

wire cutters

medium-gauge garden wire

pliers

florist's or fuse wire

raffia for hanging

■ BELOW
This fanciful little heart makes an unexpected garden detail – all the prettier because it is a surprise that so delicate a decoration should be made with ordinary garden wire.

1 Make several small heart shapes in various sizes by cutting short pieces of wire, bending them in half and curling the ends with pliers.

2 To make the large heart shape, cut a length of wire, bend it in half for the bottom of the heart and make a loop in each end. Cut a shorter length and form a loop at each end for the top. Link the looped ends to complete the outline. Lay the small hearts inside the frame as you make them, until they fill the shape.

3 Using florist's or fuse wire, bind the small hearts to the large heart and to each other where they touch, until the whole ensemble is stable. Make a hanger from raffia.

DECORATIVE GARDENER'S ACCESSORIES

In the decorative garden, there's no reason why the tools and other accoutrements used by the gardener should not be just as beautiful to look at as everything else. Gardening is always a pleasure, but it can be enhanced even further if the equipment you use has its own visual appeal. Good, well-looked-after garden tools, with handles polished with use and age, have a beauty and integrity of their own. Decorative details will beautify the rest of your gardening paraphernalia too, so that you really enjoy every task in the garden.

■ ABOVE
Decorate a ready-made apron with flower pot pockets and brass rings, to hold all your gardening essentials.

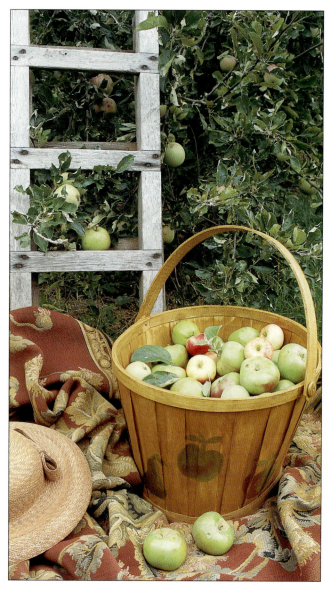

■ ABOVE
If you have fruit to pick, make the job a real pleasure by gathering it in an elegant slatted basket. This one is stencilled with images of apples and pears and given an aged look with a coat of tinted varnish.

■ ABOVE

Find your boots easily among the pile at the back door by personalizing them with charming painted designs. Just use enamel paints and take your inspiration from the garden.

■ ABOVE

You could paint an alternative design on the other boot.

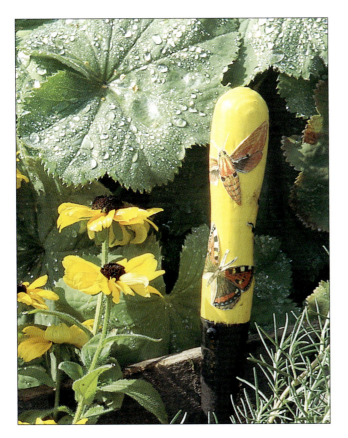

■ ABOVE

Hand tools with plain handles are easy to lose sight of in the summer border. Bright yellow paint and eye-catching insect stickers sealed with varnish make them hard to miss.

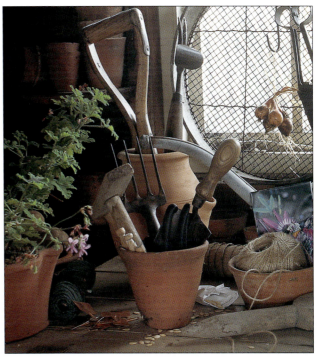

■ ABOVE

Small hand tools like trowels and forks are needed daily in the garden, so choose shapes that are comfortable to hold and a pleasure to use.

■ ABOVE

The traditional trug is a piece of garden equipment that has endured for many years and is still appreciated for its practicality, durability and fine design. Woodstains will not spoil its elegance, but they can give it individuality and provide a colour accent in the garden.

■ ABOVE

The potting shed tends to attract lots of bits and pieces, and this pretty rack will help to take care of them. Make a simple frame from lengths of garden wire and wrap a piece of chicken wire around it, binding it firmly to the frame with wire.

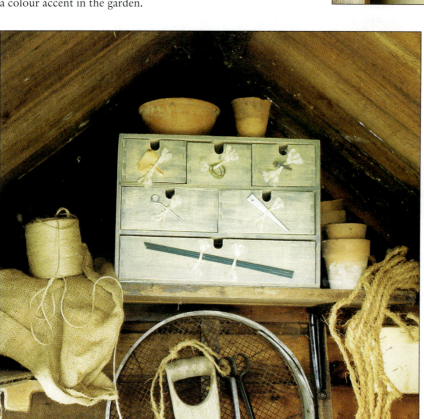

■ LEFT

Small storage drawers are handy for keeping fiddly accessories such as plant labels and rings. Label each drawer with an example of its contents so that you know exactly where they are.

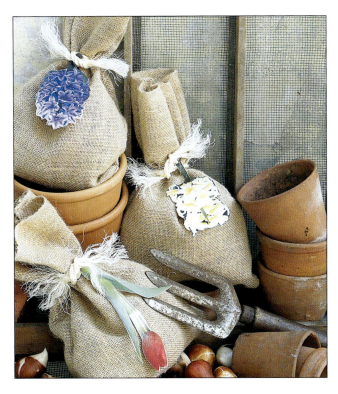

■ ABOVE
Hessian bags are useful for storing bulbs that you have lifted after flowering, as they allow the bulbs to breathe. A picture of the contents, cut from the original bulb packaging, makes the bags look good in the potting shed.

■ ABOVE
If you collect your own seeds, store them prettily in home-made paper seed packets decorated with colour photocopies of your own photographs of the flowers. This is a lovely way to give surplus seed to fellow gardeners. Write details of the plant and instructions for cultivation on the back of the packet.

■ LEFT
A wooden box with a well-fitting lid is ideal for storing half-used packets of seeds that will still be viable next season. Decoupage, using old engravings of fruit and vegetables, makes an attractive and appropriate decoration for the lid.

INDEX